BROKEN
PENCILS
STILL
WRITE

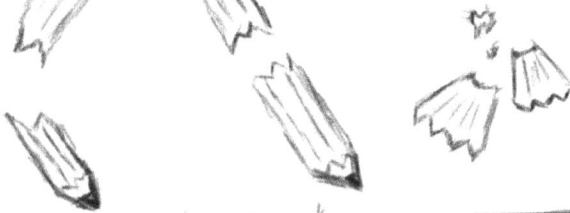

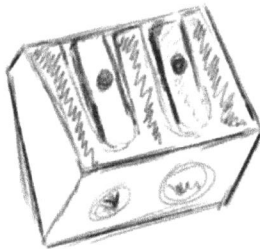

For John

Infinite gratitude and all the thanks I can say in a lifetime go to you. This book would have been impossible without your support. Everything about you is beautiful, regal, exquisite, hilarious…. magical. You took my broken pencil and helped me write in between the lines again. I owe you the universe.

For my readers

Read until your heart is full and your mind is free. I have poured my vulnerability onto these pages with purpose, so hopefully you will discover what I have recovered and find some comfort in them. Love is not a movie with safe harbors waiting for you to dock, or flooding a timeline full of pictures on social media. No, its none of those. Love is just complicated beyond measure, a power never to underestimate.

One in the morning convos....

They might not understand.
How will you know?
I'm just not sure.
Let your emotions write for you.
I can try, I just have to sharpen my pencil.

Contents

The best part of life is always the moment that you're in. Remember that bad memories are compilations soon to be your past, never to predestine your future. These words aren't meant to cut, just heal, and if they do you should cage yourself behind the bars of my thoughts. Maybe you'll finally know how it felt to be trapped, surrounded by the bare walls of your image.

Rotten Fruit

I was warned not to eat from the tree

Though the time was right, ripe for the picking
Was your fruit filled full with sweet desire?
I had to know!
They couldn't understand my hunger
The pain I felt watching, not being able to taste
Slow with torture I sat across the field of tables
I couldn't resist much more, no further
The first bite was ecstasy
The second a burst of pleasure
The third almost addiction
Then a discovery of the worst
For the core was decayed
How could I have known?
The best-looking fruit was rotten in the middle!

There was hunger in the shadows, starved for answers left and right
The questions echoed in repetition, resonating through the empty night
I drove myself to the drink of extinction, you broke my heart mid beat
She was the master who tugged your puppet strings over and over on repeat

Your lies kept their form, full of life I always believed
I was the one and only, with that, you did succeed
When she opened the door, I instantly knew
My calculations were wrong, me plus you, didn't equal two

Three minus me
It was there I poured the entirety of my entity
Giving until there was sweet nothing
To you there was no worth, to me you were still everything

I severed myself in half to make you whole
There in that barren side of my closet I lost my soul
You ran into abyss, I finally discovered the answers I sought
Those tears that fell, I never fought

Got no more soul in my shoes
No more color in my blues
Tears that produce waterfalls
Rivers that bend when the sea calls

What I got left
After this heart theft?

Got no more latitude in my height
Tell me I'm wrong for being right
Try and direct the play as sadness sings
With my broken heart strings

What I got left
After this heart theft?

I paid all my dues and fines
Except for the debt in between these lines
Lost all the records of the good times
Yet you got every detail of my misdeeming crimes

What I got left
After this heart theft?

Why did you give me pieces taken, that you disturbed?
Sacred from foundation you specifically built for her?
A construction once cherished, you deferred
To revisit after it was I, you lustfully observed

Have you ever truly touched her?
Without intentions dampened, full of sin
The truth, the lies, the indifference
Unknown to humankind, deep delved within?

Her beauty is only one that I can fathom
Internally she must assert rightful demand
An equation beyond your cerebral container
Hundreds of reasons in addition of why her sum is grand

Do not think of me less than that of a queen
I reign this kingdom from the bottoms of my heel
To the tops of my wavy strands
Nothing of who I am I dare not conceal

I deny you to ruin my forthcoming
Full of promise, proper and pristine
Nor could you ever have my hand, again
Yours were never clean

Never will you ruin me, like you have ruined her.

There will never be rest in the abysmal
A century of stupor, a tortuous perennial
Soaked drunk with regret, a thirst not meant to quench
Hunger of a beast not satisfied until dispense

Consider me foolish to follow
To the depths of despair
There is not a place discovered
Where I would not pursue you there

No body of interest
No sight would please more
No promise of wealth
No feeling more sore

It was a start to an end
As soon as your arrival
Clenched between my fingers
A smidgen of hope for survival

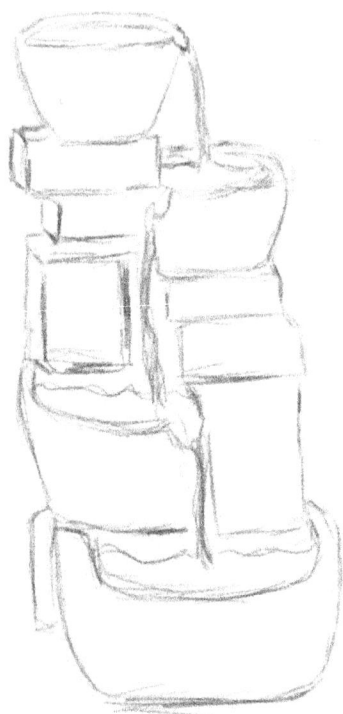

This pain in full,
I have paid in full
Balanced to straighten lines
Crooked in symmetry

In this awkward stage
Transitioning from whole to half
The wealth once had
On this dirt road, dirt broke

Still there is an infinite beauty
Smothering, solemn sadness
In a race of slothful torment
Consuming me without consent

Drinking from my fountain
Keeping close immortality
What poison!!
You, filthy poison, almost my fatality

What happens to a love deferred waiting to proceed?
I think of you often, weeks of saddened forecast
Tears falling form the condensing clouds
Waiting for a ray of shine from the dimmed sun

It's just so…complicated!

Why can't you hold me anyway?

These were my favorite glasses from a time before
Improperly used to see the less turned to more
I had visions prior, none that gave 20/20
Responsibility did not introduce, in time to save me

The defined intention of first initial see and need
I took a slice of offer, consumed into your greed
Your timid soul I devoured, taste of bitter sweet
Desire fulfilled to the brim, that smile, our greet

Vulnerable to weakness I had to travel foot and bare
To distant miles, aimless, no question or care
You hid the worst so well, wrapped with a smile
A beast that took the beauty, turned to vicious vile

My eyes never checked, a prescription I lacked from start
You gave me all of your anatomy, except your heart
First, I was the fool, to put you in favor before all else
Gaze into the mirror put these glasses on yourself

Release Me!

This will be the last of many
Your grip no longer tight around the bare
Your love no longer lingers
Our love no longer there

Time could not be measured
No matter the effort forth
The value that once was
Exist in past tense, a memory of sort

There is no question left
A love denies deferred
Moved on to greater worth
Your heart belongs to her

I ditto this same remark
With no intention for future envy
Carry with you the closure sought
I rest in peace with what could be

A goodbye holds its substance
A hello is the start of my new
There was once upon a time
Now there's me, no longer a need for you

You wondered exactly how much
I cared?
I barely said good morning,
Only to say good night
To a ghost that only wanted
A body to host when no one else would
Entertain
I gave you all my riches
You spared me change
I begged you for infinity
You gave me a fraction of a second
I asked for it all in return
Finally, you gave me back, myself

Selfish of me to admit a true, yet outlandish fact
Which justifies how much you've lacked
I'm left wishing that I could have found him inside of you
You didn't have the courage to see it through
The core of my dispute is held in the nuclei of my beating
heart
Our differences have driven us to opposing poles driving
us apart
The concerns of yesterday with thoughts of tomorrow in
mind
Depletes the sweet sugar rush of anticipation left bitter
behind
I have loved you without limit surpassing the reach of
infinite space
Beauty is not held in the eyes on a massive search from
face to face
I would know, when I swam through the sea of masks,
each a hidden soul
You were the only one I could penetrate through seeing
you as a whole
I would have rather ate off your plate on a constant record
of use
Instead of displaying you like a plate of fine china,
falsifying the truth
Each day was a day where our troublesome disputes could
have been forgiven
Yet we carried the burden of our differences underneath
our smiles hidden
I have often thought back of how happiness once
infiltrated our minds
Penetrated each other's flaws and contracted our hearts
into pocket size shrines

So everywhere we went they would beat in unison in the palm of our hands

The whisper of your thoughts tossed in the air lost in my hair strands

I was the tick you were the tock, the pendulum of love swaying back and forth

Eloquently moved in motion toward forward time, bought not borrowed- long but short

The concept of time being so insufficient in the matters of love and relations

Not once did you ever believe that it could ever be so sudden, losing all sensations

Bridged apart, I think it's safe to say that it's time to burn our trails

At the light house you remain, as I ready to set my sails

Freedom!

I used to believe in fairytales too

The arrangement of breakfast in bed
Laying in an assortment of rose petals spread
Taking time to make time
Slow it down a notch just to say "you're mine"

I used to believe in fairytales too

When your heart was an open door
Summer warmth by the sea shore
Always a hunger that was never satisfied
Protection and comfort that you would provide

I used to believe in fairytales too

Until the wall we built crumbled down around us
Sitting on top of wasted trust
I watch the horizon of new beginnings
Picking up traces of heart trimmings

Do you still believe in fairy tales too?

I am not a request
For any need
I am not a page in your chapter
For a good read
I am not a woman bounced off the rim
For you to rebound
I am the forever you can't have
The lost waiting to be found

How deceptive of you to make me believe
Every notion of fallacy up your sleeve
I demand the truth or a dare to lie
Give me liberty or let me die

Surmounted on the heap of regret
I watch the eye of the storm form a stage to set
The rage of nature into a hurricane of hate
Spiral uncontrollably coming together to congregate

While we separate to destroy instead
You choose to be dictated and lead
There must be freedom to decide
Cowardice actions you shelter and hide

You follow this plan, instead of the flow
The finale of this amusement show

I cry NOT
because I am weak
because I am alone
because I am lonely
because I am worthless
because of all the reasons
that you ALMOST
convinced me to believe

I cry NOW
Because I am happy
Because I have been shown
Only I can save myself, but now
There's no one to save YOU!

Finally, I have been released.

Recovery

Undress me with your hands
Cold from the glass mixed with jack
Do not stare in my eyes
This is not a search, but a rescue

Your value is numeric
Tattooed into the skin of wood
Plunge into the shallow
Come up only for needed air

Count the hours few
I cannot promise a tomorrow
Leave my door slight ajar
See yourself to exit as you did upon enter

You were never meant for a term,
No longer than a month worth
The warmth that you provided
T 'was a night gently placed near a burning hearth

You whispered a name that your heart spoke
Dare not to speak of mine
It might be her that you love
For the evening, I take place and time

Confuse me for all your wanting
As long as I am free at day
These nights of tender longings
Only a few needed of your lonely nights to stay

These deeds dirty, distress to a raging damsel
Downward despair, pieces of disport spread across
A field of bloom drenched with 90% proof
Sparked into wildfire, where her head was laid

Where are you now, knight in dulled armor?

She sleeps with the untamed, only in shadows of dark
A veil to cover the wounds exposed
So, you won't be able to see the severity
Damned if you ever have the best of her sullen soul

The few that will ever love
Will be the few that will break her tender psyche
The many that will taste
Will be the many that will never forget

All that I could offer
Will be of your taking tonight
Deep in its end, a soul that wander
Dive into me, until you find light

Sulky streams serenading
On my ominous path
Forgo the thoughts
Feel only passion, succumb of wrath

Taste me slowly
Take me fast
Do not torment
You are not my first, nor the last

I mold his body
Envisioned to fit yours
Another etched into my skin
Another less of nothing more

Roses by the garden that grow blood red
Panama made, Brooklyn bred
Violets bloom with a hint of rhythm and blue
Present in this garden an addiction that grows for you

Benny you be bumping my heart strings kid!
I speak so fluent, but with you speech is limited
Swag & class infused in the entity of one man
Free of restraint and formal plan

Even if this world may not understand
The time between us spread far in between
You remain in the distance as memory
To be thought often, revisited in dreams

L
  O
    V
      E is?

Annoying
Bashful
Catastrophic
Demanding
Everything
Forgiving
Gratitude
Honest
Integrity
John
Kind
Learning
Meaning
Naked
Open
Promise
Quarrels
Random
Silent
Tough
Unstable
Vibrant
Wonder
X-tra
Yearning
Zesty

Instead of exchanging love faces
Let's get lost in each other's empty spaces
Euphoric, climaxing into ecstasy
With the use of a metaphor or a simple simile
I have you in my rapture
Get to the level of my stature
So we can see eye to eye
The speed of time can fly
The guard to my heart is lowering the gate
But the guard to my brain stands firm in debate
My password to my brain has a password
Please don't talk that nonsense and don't be absurd
I know the game because I've played each side
I've won, I've lost, and I've tied
I've left the court
Now I sit in the bleachers watching others get cut short
I'm not asking for promises that can be broken
Or a "sure thing" that can be stolen
Just the effort and the determination
For us to be something more than a lustful hallucination
More than ready to give this ride a try
I'll happily tell the last dealer my final goodbye

For the price of one embrace
I would have molded the world to fit
Into the palm of your hands
Offered you all that was in it

There was no climb
No mile untraveled
No ocean depth too deep
No secret left to unravel

I fed no reasons
To distrust a bone inside
A body that would only lie
In the ground than to tell what you confide

Still I will always be the last pluck
From the flower
…..he loves me
He loves me not.

I drink till I am empty
I cry till I am sane
I wish it all be different
I try to forget your name

Still, I couldn't hate you.

Revive
Me

Hate, My dearest

I have no knowledge of your ways or motives alike
Yet we are similar as genetics entwined tightly like destiny
would have it
We have crossed paths and danced alongside each other in
romance
Why must you deny me in the wake of day and times of
rest in tranquil darkness?

What pleasure it must be to watch others mourn in your
presence
What delight it must bring to hear the down pour from the
eyes of the storm
What satisfaction is it to you my dear because I have never
tasted such a passion fruit
Tell me of it all I must know, I beg for peace and you want
for war

There is such warmth in the youth of newfound adoration
Free of biased opinion, proven without harsh perils of
objectivity
The tenderness of a child's touch where innocence is first
born
The laughter at their own ignorance, a kiss of bliss from
cupid's bow

I give unannounced, and render my hand free of any
expected return
An embrace well needed after news of catastrophic events
Loyal to the purity of joy, evoking only the happiness
when sadness pushes her aside

I have done the same for each soul that has suffered for me in my name

My virtue has been planted by the hand ALMIGHTY, the seeds of patience
I invite you to taste the sweet of my fruits, after all I have tasted your bitter
Even when the downpour occurs, know that I will be the one to wipe them clear
My dearest Hate, I will always endure

Respectfully not yours,

Love

Life is once, mistakes are many
GO forth in distance though doubt may thrive
The journey will service your expected bounty
We are given the choice of will while alive

There may be hate, let it fester
There may be scorn, let them talk
There may be failure, let it be
When there is change, learn the walk

This world spins in motion tilted at axis
As the people scurry in frantic direction
I choose to stand, while others blend
Into a crowd that cares only of social perfection

If you dare be you, many will follow suite
Knit the unique sequence of your style tight to stitch
Into your skin and sink your message into your bone
Embrace the difference that you've sown

My heart beats quiet, the night is at rest while stars sing
In distant space my thoughts linger with Saturn's ring
I search the difference between the days depart
There is not much, only light and dark

It comes swift, as nostalgia consumes my body whole
It is there I stay, my imprisoned soul
Leave me, spare my life for another chance
That once again someone may love my broken stance

I offer ruins, MY RUINS from faults of my own
They are embedded into the deep, I wear what I have
sown
If you could still have me for what is left
I have lost the most through petty theft

We live in these hours, 24 at a time, how should we spend?
With each that passes, we come closer to a nearer end
Our souls are wild, not meant to be tamed
Just guided through the halls of faces, that wish not to be
named

My hands would be left empty, if you should choose
another
They are meant for yours, no less, no more, no other
In my journey you will always remain
A constant thought adrift in the wind, sand and grain

Try and bear with me my dearest when our love seeks no
further growth
Sunlight is absent and we are left with a stem of broken
oath
Our hands no longer play or mingle the way lovers should
The beautiful and tragic loss of innocence we have given
up to adulthood

I ask you, do you remember the times of endless longing

The curiosity, the lessons taught, and the purpose of us
learning?
I don't want to have to beg for memories, for you to be
reminded
We reviewed our original oath, read it out loud, and
verbally signed it

I know that we are both lost seeking different paths
 We were once a whole now we're separated in halves
Distributing the peace once had, we answer "yes" to a call
on war
No attempt from you to make a treaty, civil to settle the
score

You may call me selfish for trying to save this severed love
I'll try and correct your vision where push comes to shove
I'm the optometrist, let me come in contact with you
Tell me, is it better one or two?

There is no simple way or plan of remedy
To ask you to recite our song from ancient memory
So, try and bear with me my dearest, hold on steadfast
Let us consolidate our vision of the future with a collage
from the past

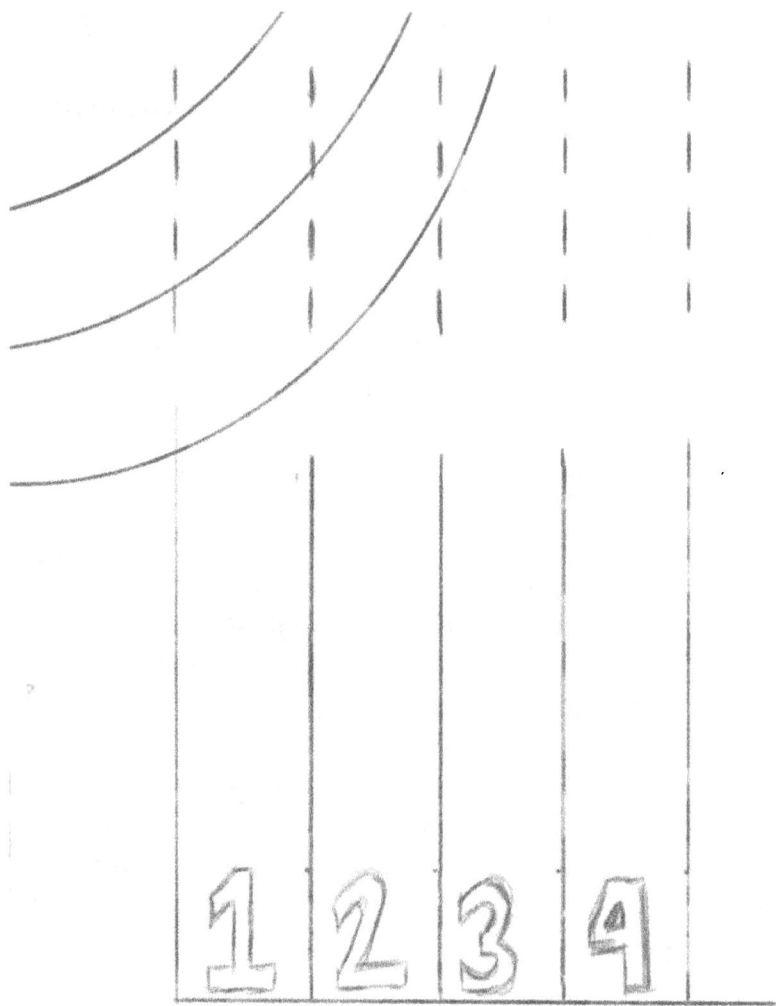

I have answers that I wish to attain
I want to hold you as close as my heart can bear
Your questionable answers leave me in strain
I'm afraid that I'll fall into your mysterious stare

I run in circle that surround the seams and thread
Wy do you turn and watch me knowing I want you?
The track and field of waving misery inside my head
Running drudgingly step after step, just see me through

I promise to have you and hold you until time fades
I hold on to the memories that already happened
Through the health of or youth to the wisdom of old age
Hoping for more borrowed time to have, leaves my soul
saddened

Do you ever lose yourself when you hear my name?
Terrified, I must risk in order for you to know
Do you believe that if we go wild, we could ever be tame?
I want to tell you everything and give my all to show

Don't rush a thing, just promise you'll hold my hand
Take off my cool and I'll take off yours
A minute without you is one I can't stand
Opportunities of happiness through these closed doors

These are bare walls
Meant to shelter me
With warmth, blankets thick with understanding
Some hours are spent on others,
Needs that fulfill ours
I do it all to playback
To my cave of bare walls

JRD

Without you I would not have known
The worth of my intellect beyond my anatomy
What a waste of your time
The worst part is how much I still consigned

Fought, I should have fought!
The nights where you were up wondering
Why my love was immature,
I wanted more than what I could handle
I always ran back when I wasn't sure

This apology is meant for you
I do not wish it all back
Just a thank you for all
The memories that will be the best
Love from the spring, down to the fall

I am truly sorry

Let me hold charity for another day
To visit remembrance once or twice
To pause the rewind of the best scene
Call my name and I yours, till it suffices
Fickle wanting change as seasons do, I stay same
Dreaming in the morning, tossing in tides of sheets
Dragging me to shore back to where I started
The beacon blown to ashes, I turn my cheek
Forever was the limit that our journey reached

My heart, my heart
Formed as a picture of art
I painted one masterpiece
And you are my next start
Your flawless stride
My feelings guide
Gravitating towards you
Feelings anew!!!

Finally, I can fly without wings
Against natural law, impossible things
Every record of pain searing through my insides
Memory to rewind back to the place it resides

Death is not a monogamist, he takes several at times
Only this once I've been revived
I will take this risk for I have been granted
A chance that many may never see
A path I would have never traveled
Not by land, or sky, nor by sea

Rightfully
Yours

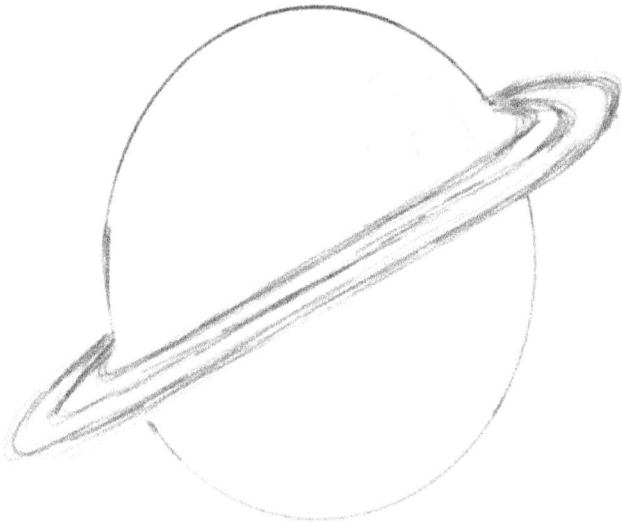

Our mind full of wonder as it wanders
A random thought that shoots and saunters
Round and round the rings of debris and crust
Saturn's ring don't got a thing on us

Every bit a pixel of perfect, we consolidate
Together we stand still, pure 100% no concentrate
We follow the road less taken without guides
No map of what lies ahead, no planned strides

Memories that threaten and sting
Voices we both remember, let free to ring
This journey has been the longest one
For the longest you've been the only one

The time is now or never
A time of prosper, last past forever
Hollow be thy frame
Every syllable, every letter to your name

J-O-H-N

Bond us until we are one, unbreakable in spirit as time grows old
Out of mystery we discover, under scrutiny we defy the hand forced to fold
The pressures days may form, into the heat of arguments that tailor us close to bone
What could be under the rugged rubble of pebbles and stone?

You're a want of many desires, so I hope only mine will do
My words may Cut, but only for truth to emerge in all its glory for you
It is I, who will know the difference over the greed that constructs from lust
From atoms of carbon in ratio to our anatomy risen from ashes, fallen to dust

Adornment is the cause, blood shed is the forgotten effect
Deep in the mantle underneath our surfaced skin, beauty is imbedded to protect
It is not for the world to grasp, only to see for eyes transparent beyond cosmetic touch
In its purest image love is made tangible after matured existence, careful coordination is such

My love we are forever solid in 1 Carat, whatever that span may weigh in measure
Grams of envy, inches close to madness, or intimate fires of Fahrenheit exploding in pleasure
DIAMONDS ARE FOREVER- no amount of weathered storm can deteriorate our passion
It seemed as if millions of years have passed to make us present, dressed in ultimate fashion

So precious you are to me, I wish to adore you with one that is just as unique
The adjustment to my views where guided by your wisdom, vision left conformed, concrete
This world could never understand or come close to comprehend our bond of genuine feat
WE ARE FOREVER, so pair my love with yours as one, only you will make me complete

COLOR
CLARITY
CARAT
CUT

Your grapes are bold, aged red of wine
Your taste a coat that shields all others
I risk my hours for a minute of time
That you may glance for a mere second

Your cheek brushed blush into shade of rose
Your eyes depths of ocean blue,
The relief was effort less than given
My bounty offered unto you

Forever will feel like an instant
As an image taken will surely paint
To capture a moment for eternity
Memory will harbor, though it will be faint

2

+

2

=

Pythagorean's amended love theory

Faith squared
+
Hope Squared
=
Love infinitely

I long to know what your heart desires
From the peak of dawn to dusk expired
Turning orbit, a planet full of hopeless race
Crowning convenience to quicken useless pace
Let us unite and form a structured union of reality
For you were once a dream, turned to actuality
Where there is hope, there is love, and where there is love, there is us
A place even eternity couldn't touch
For some it is illusion, not talk of such
I yell from the mount of Everest, and drown in the deepest blue
Wherever this journey will take, I pray to the heavens it leads me to you

You're beautiful in a different kind of way
Not in the length of your hair or the trim of your brow
You're smart in a different kind of way
When I'm short of words you finish statements, my mouth
could not allow

You glow in a different kind of way
Surrounded in 50 shades of the dullest gray yet you give
me the purest image
You captivate me in a different kind of way
Torn in between an illusion of want and need the most
difficult scrimmage

I care for you in a different kind of way
One that is superior above any need or selfish desire
I yearn for you in a different kind of way
Unlike any that I have ever courted, every feeling
transpired

Your humor is unique in a different kind of way
Dry as a straw of wheat with a smidgen of wit
Yet you still make me laugh in a different kind of way
The air never stiff, always warm as I breathe in every bit

I hope you can love me just as different in the same kind of
way
For all the reasons I could ever list eternally
I will always feel the same in a different kind of way
Till the day our verdict heard, my love will flow endlessly

Standing in the midnight shadows that secluded the sleuth
You wear a veil of envy and distrust that covers the truth
Don't try and hide you past mistakes
Your regrets, misjudgments, or sorrowful intakes

As a true agent of love, I seek genuine compassion
A form fitting outfit styled in every fashion
Although I may never reach perfection
I will receive the respect and affection

This is what I have always deserved
A place in one's man's heart permanently reserved
A trial without the jury no need for a judge
Prosecute my heart for being in love

Your past may not be ready to let you go
But if you'd let me I would like to proceed the show
Tell me if it's ever too much to ask
Your hand in mine hooked to clasp

We have come to exist in flesh for reasons beyond our rationality
Our destiny is not planned, but lived in accordance with our decisions
I hope that I was a decision you made in whole heart
This journey of purpose is one I want to travel, only with you

May I ask to become an impartial thought in all that you desire?
Withstanding seasons that may challenge our future to come
I will bear your name, as you may own my heart
An eternity to solve your mystery with a second of your permission

"I do" take you for your simplicity in complex situations
When anger controls your actions, and your frustrations weigh down on your abilities
When happiness reigns at your peak, and sadness encompasses your emotions
In health when your energy defies gravity, and in sickness when your best is at your least

My chances are none, for the fish in the sea will never be a proper compare
A love is formed with careful nourishment & sacrifice when deemed appropriate
You will always be my ONE, not to be confused in the mass of natural numbers
In life we shall ne'er part, in death we will meet again, for you are the alpha and the omega

You share with me your worth
Without an inquiry of any need
You take sweet nothings well received
No ounce of pity, no trace of greed

Piles of prayers that came late night
I whispered solemnly underneath
Clouds that poured down my iniquities
You gathered every inch of filthy sheath

Revealed my naked essence, a suppressed truth
Showered me clean, until you earned
The entirety of me, still broken of a whole
Only God could have trusted you for my soul's return

For this I thank you, now I know
Each that came before, anticipating doors
No other key was made for my lock
For I was always intended to be rightfully yours!

This is just the beginning

Possibilities are journeys with multiple destinations, there are no true restrictions, just ones that you feed to your own fear. For the longest time I've suppressed my feelings and have tried to erase the past, but now I'm sitting here with a blank canvas trying to create a future. How can I? It wouldn't be possible without the portraits of my past. Lord, continue to bless me. I'm still standing.

www.ingramcontent.com/pod-product-compliance
Lightning Source LLC
Chambersburg PA
CBHW031539040426
42445CB00010B/620